Batik

W9-AZH-331

Batik

20 Beautiful Projects Using Simple Techniques

DIANA LIGHT

LARK BOOKS

A Division of Sterling Publishing Co., Inc.
New York

Editor: Valerie Van Arsdale Shrader
Art Director: Dana Margaret Irwin
Photographer: Sandra Stambaugh
Cover Designer: Barbara Zaretsky
Assistant Art Director: Hannes Charen
Production Assistance: Laura Gabris
Editorial Assistance: Delores Gosnell, Anne Wolfe Hollyfield, Rosemary Kast

10 9 8 7 6 5 4 3 2 1

First Edition

Published by Lark Books, a division of
Sterling Publishing Co., Inc.
387 Park Avenue South, New York, N.Y. 10016

© 2004, Lark Books

Distributed in Canada by Sterling Publishing,
c/o Canadian Manda Group, One Atlantic Ave., Suite 105
Toronto, Ontario, Canada M6K 3E7

Distributed in the U.K. by Guild of Master Craftsman Publications Ltd., Castle Place,
166 High Street, Lewes, East Sussex, England
BN7 1XU
Tel: (+ 44) 1273 477374, Fax: (+ 44) 1273 478606, Email:
pubs@thegmcgroup.com, Web: www.gmcpublications.com

Distributed in Australia by Capricorn Link (Australia) Pty Ltd.,
P.O. Box 704, Windsor, NSW 2756 Australia

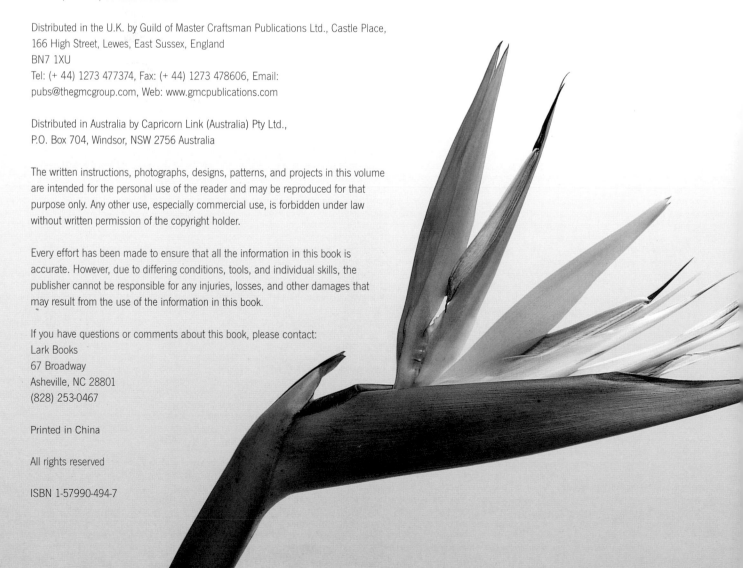

The written instructions, photographs, designs, patterns, and projects in this volume
are intended for the personal use of the reader and may be reproduced for that
purpose only. Any other use, especially commercial use, is forbidden under law
without written permission of the copyright holder.

Every effort has been made to ensure that all the information in this book is
accurate. However, due to differing conditions, tools, and individual skills, the
publisher cannot be responsible for any injuries, losses, and other damages that
may result from the use of the information in this book.

If you have questions or comments about this book, please contact:
Lark Books
67 Broadway
Asheville, NC 28801
(828) 253-0467

Printed in China

All rights reserved

ISBN 1-57990-494-7

CONTENTS

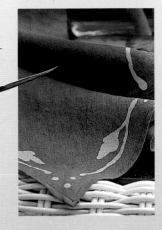

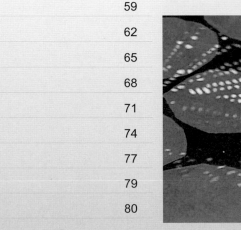

This traditional batik, made by the Maio in China, demonstrates fine craftsmanship and intricate design. Garment from the collection of Mary S. Parker.

INTRODUCTION

Batik is an ancient process. At its heart, it's a very simple technique: wax resists dye and blocks it from fabric, revealing a design underneath when the wax is removed. For more than 2,000 years, various cultures have decorated cloth with batik, and today the art continues to flourish. Modern batik can be an easy, elegant way to express your creativity. In this book, it's presented as a very accessible craft, one you can learn in a weekend and use to produce simply beautiful—and beautifully simple—designs for yourself and your home. Unlike the traditional fabrics that were intricate works of art produced over many months, the projects in this book make it easy to learn to batik by streamlining the basic process. Using found objects like spools and wooden blocks lends a contemporary feel to the designs.

Batik allows you the opportunity to indulge yourself in design and color; what a thrill it is to see the patterns emerge in the dyebath! And you may be surprised to learn that you don't need many specialized tools, much less a dedicated workshop, to get started in batik. A trip to the craft store for dye, wax, and tools; a brief stop at a discount store for plastic tubs; and you'll be ready to begin.

Contemporary batik is bright and exciting.

If you love textiles, this is the perfect craft for you, because a whole range of natural fabrics including cotton, linen, rayon, and silk is suitable for batik. Many of the projects in the book use "blanks," or undyed articles like scarves and pillow covers. Others require just a little quick sewing—a seam or a hem here and there—to create stylish home accessories such as simple slipcovers. The surface designs themselves are the focus of the book, and I'll teach you how to use common, everyday items like cookie cutters and dowels to create distinctive patterns you can translate onto virtually any item you choose. Of course, I also show you how to use a tjanting, or wax pen, the traditional tool of batik.

You'll choose from lots of fabulous ideas when you're deciding on your first project. Want a special swimsuit for a tropical getaway? It's on page 28. How about a cool lunch bag to wow your coworkers? Look at page 22. Need some pillows to spruce up an old couch? Try page 26 or page 48. A card for a certain someone? Page 71. There are 21 great projects for you and your home, all easy and fun.

Though steeped in tradition, batik is also exciting and contemporary. When you're creating the projects in this book, I hope you enjoy your exploration into this modern approach to a timeless craft.

Blue was the predominant color of traditional batik, shown here in a design by the Hmong of Thailand. Fabric from the collection of Mary S. Parker.

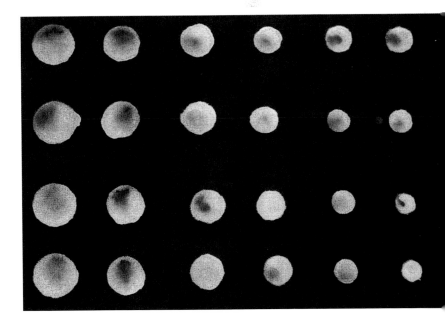

An everyday object like a spool can be used to create modern designs.

A BRIEF HISTORY

Who discovered that wax resists dye? Where was it, and when? No one is sure. Remnants of linen decorated with batik were found in Egyptian tombs dating from the fifth century A.D., and excavations in China reveal that batik was definitely practiced there in the seventh century A.D. Some evidence points to China as the source of the craft, as early as the first or second century B.C., with its spread likely occurring through trade routes like the famous Silk Road. Ancient examples of batik were also found in Japan and India, where batik was done on cotton rather than silk.

At some point, probably the twelfth or thirteenth century A.D., the craft reached the islands of Indonesia, where it was embraced and refined. The peoples of Java, in particular, developed the process into a fine art, and it remains vitally important as an artistic medium as well as a major industry on the island. The Javanese added a

significant innovation—the *tjanting*—a pen with a reservoir to hold hot wax. The development of this tool allowed the artist to create more intricate designs by actually drawing with wax, while the first examples of batik had been patterns created by small dots of wax.

Other cultures throughout the ancient world practiced resist dyeing. Because beeswax was plentiful in many areas, it became the logical resist, but some civilizations used different substances. In Africa, rice paste, cassava paste (derived from a root plant), and mud were all used as resists. Early dyes came from natural materials, too; the indigo plant yielded the traditional blue so often seen in batik. On Java, the bark of the soga tree made a lovely dye that ranged in color from yellow to brown. Leaves and roots of various plants offered more hues.

The Dutch introduced batik to Europe in the seventeenth century A.D., after they colonized Java. In the early 1800s, several European countries attempted to mass-produce batiked fabrics, with some success. In response, the Javanese developed yet another innovation, the *tjap*. The tjap, an intricate stamp made of copper, allowed the craftsperson to print designs on fabric rather than use the more time-consuming tjanting. This method proved to be efficient and economical and allowed the Javanese to reclaim the industry as more expensive European

At right, examples of traditional batik dress; below, young girls in Bali use the tjanting to create designs in the early 1900s. Images from the collection of Mary S. Parker.

Bârâ Boedoer. *Java, April 13th 1908* Batikster.

production declined. Modern batiks from Java are created primarily using this method, while more traditional *tulis* batiks made with the tjanting are still produced, though they're expensive to purchase.

Today you can see the influence of batik everywhere, from haute couture to the linens section of the department store. But you don't have to settle for what the marketplace offers you—you can make your own batik! It's not necessary that you be trained in the fine arts to use resist dyeing to produce beautiful surface design. Learn about the tools (and tricks) of the trade in the following section.

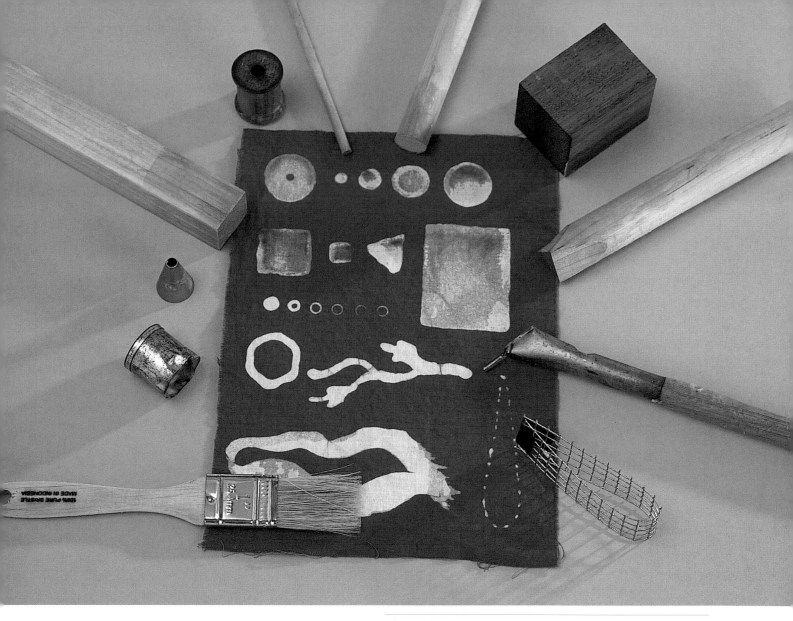

BATIK BASICS

Simple batik isn't a difficult process, though it does have several distinct steps—waxing, dyeing, and finishing. Before I talk about the uncomplicated tabletop batik techniques I use, let's discuss the tools and materials, so you understand the supplies you'll be using when you work.

Tools

TJANTING. I've already mentioned the traditional tjanting, the wax pen, pictured at the right. At its simplest, it consists of a metal bowl (probably brass) mounted on a wooden stem with a spout. Tjantings are available with different size spouts, and you can switch between them depending on the degree of detail you need in your design. There are also tjantings with multiple spouts, and electrical models, too.

When you work, you dip the tjanting into the hot wax, fill the bowl with it, and draw the design. Most sources will tell you to hold the tjanting just like a writing pen; I suggest that you experiment with the tool a bit first before you begin your first piece. Read more about using the tjanting on page 14. If you're the slightest bit intimidated by this tool, don't fret, because you can also use simple stamps to create beautiful motifs.

STAMPS. Surprisingly enough, many everyday items can create sophisticated designs on fabric. An old spool, a wooden dowel, a folded piece of cardboard, a cookie cutter—all these found objects are wonderful tools for batik.

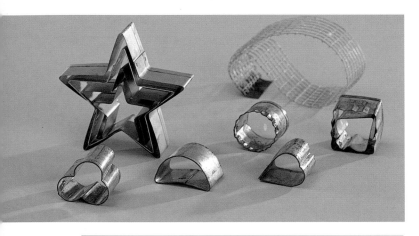

Cookie cutters make great stamps, but you can also make your own. Learn how to make the paisley shape, shown in the background, on page 49.

Wooden dowels are excellent stamping tools.

Basically, you can try any item that won't melt in hot wax, so metal and wooden items are perfect.

BRUSHES. You can also apply wax with brushes, and they're very helpful in filling in large designs that you may have outlined with a tjanting or a stamp. But you can also draw and create interesting effects with brushes. Those with stiff natural bristles seem to be best for batik. I also used artist's brushes to paint dye onto a few projects.

ELECTRIC SKILLET. For melting wax, get an electric skillet with temperature control and dedicate it to batik. An economical alternative is a simple double boiler; if you really get turned on to batik, consider investing in a specialized wax pot. I liked the electric skillet that I used for this book; once I got familiar with its operation, it worked like a charm and was extremely reliable.

PLASTIC TUBS. I used five of these inexpensive containers for dyeing, boiling, and rinsing. The largest tub in my collection was 32 x 19 x 15^1/$_2$ inches (81 x 48 x 39 cm); the very smallest, a clear tub, was 13^1/$_2$ x 8 x 4 inches (34 x 20 x 10 cm). Choose a container that allows your item to float freely so it dyes evenly; this also helps avoid *crackling*, discussed in the section on wax below. Wide containers are better than narrow ones for tabletop batik. You can also use vessels made from other materials, such as glass, enamel, and stainless steel, if you have them on hand.

MEASURING TOOLS. You'll need spoons, cups, and pitchers to measure the ingredients in the dyebath—dye, salt, washing soda, and water.

WOODEN SPOONS OR TONGS. Use these tools to stir the dyebath, manipulate the items in the dye, and remove pieces from the tubs.

JARS WITH LIDS. Round up all your old preserve jars to mix dye. Be sure the lids fit tightly before you start mixing!

SILK PINS. Several of the projects use these pins to secure the fabric onto a frame. The silk pins hold the fabric taut while it's being decorated.

Materials

WAX. Three kinds of wax can be used for batik. Natural beeswax is the traditional resist; it's soft, penetrates the fabric well, and blocks dye thoroughly. Synthetic microcrystalline wax offers many of the advantages of beeswax—it's pliable and penetrates fabric easily, but has a high flash point, so it can be more easily heated to higher temperatures. Paraffin is thinner than either of the other options, and tends to crack, which leads to an effect called, obviously enough, crackling, wherein the dye seeps

through the wax to form fine lines of color on the white design. Some crackling may occur naturally in batik, though traditional batik was to be free of cracks. Today, some artists work to enhance this effect rather than eliminate it. Crackling is minimized in the projects in this book, but it's easy to achieve by crumpling the item before you place it in the dyebath.

Your personal preference may lead you to choose one wax product over the other. For my money (literally), microcrystalline wax is the way to go. It's affordable and effective; I created all of the projects in this book with it. You'll learn more about the application of wax, as well as important safety tips, later in this chapter.

DYE. For the best results, use cold-water, fiber-reactive dyes. Because they don't require hot water, the wax won't erode while the article is being dyed. These powder dyes, produced by several different manufacturers, produce rich, colorfast shades. Sodium chloride (salt) and sodium carbonate (washing soda) are also needed for the dye process. The chemical composition of these elements in the dyebath creates an actual bond with the fiber; see the sidebar at right for an explanation of how and why these dyes work. Theoretically, you can use other kinds of dye, but you should keep their working properties in mind. For example, you can't use a dye that requires boiling water to activate, or it will remove the wax before the article is dyed. If you use a dye that's not colorfast when it's subjected to the boiling water in the wax removal process, the color may disappear. So you have to remove the wax by ironing instead of boiling.

WHICH DYES?

*C*old-water, fiber-reactive dyes are the choice of batik artists. This dye family produces a superior result because the process creates a chemical bond in the fiber itself, so the dye becomes a part of the fiber rather than merely staining the surface. Because the dye works in cold water, it's perfect for batik, because the wax must remain intact during the entire dye process. (Hot water will, of course, melt the wax.) And in truth, "cold" water is a little misleading, as most of the dyes are actually mixed with lukewarm water.

For the scientifically minded, here's how fiber-reactive dyes work:

In addition to the dye and water, salt is added to the mixture. The salt encourages the dye to adhere to the fabric; it creates an electrostatic charge that pushes the color into the cloth. Sodium carbonate (in the form of washing soda or soda ash) makes it all happen, because it raises the pH of the water. This activates and fixes the dye, making the color permanent. For another important tip about purchasing dye, see What Do The Symbols Mean? on page 19.

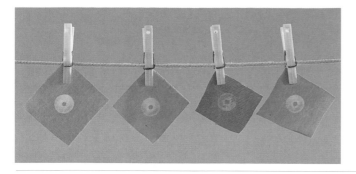

Each of these swatches has a different fiber content. All of them were stamped with the same tool and left in the same dyebath for the same period of time, but note the difference in appearance. In the photo at the left, from left to right, the fabrics are cotton, white cotton duck, unbleached canvas, and cotton knit; in the photo at the right, from left to right, linen, silk chiffon, hemp/silk blend, and silk crêpe de Chine. This dye was also used on pages 32 and 59.

SODIUM CHLORIDE. This is plain old table salt. Use the non-iodized variety.

SODIUM CARBONATE. I used washing soda as this agent. Be sure to purchase your washing soda at a craft store, because the brands available at the grocery store may have additives (like bleach) that interfere with the batik process.

FABRIC. Fiber-reactive dyes can be used with great success on all of the following: cotton, linen, rayon, silk, and a luscious fabric that is a blend of hemp and silk that I found at my specialty fabric shop. While some sources recommend making changes in the basic dye formula for a protein-based fabric like silk, I found that no tinkering was necessary. But fabrics are affected differently by dye depending on their fiber content, as the photos above demonstrate. For more information on fabric and clothing blanks, also see Which Fabrics Work? on page 13.

You may know that you can't use synthetic fabrics or synthetic blends with any degree of success, as they won't absorb dye satisfactorily.

LAUNDRY AND DISHWASHING DETERGENT. Fabric or garment blanks must first be laundered before you begin working, to remove any excess oils or finishes. Then you'll wash them again after the batik process is complete. The dishwashing liquid helps remove residue during the wax removal procedure.

RUBBER AND FABRIC GLOVES. Be sure to wear rubber gloves when you're working with dye. You'll also need some fabric gloves to protect your hands when you're using warm stamps. I also wore an old pair of fabric gloves beneath my rubber gloves while I was boiling out the wax, but you might look for a pair of insulated rubber gloves instead.

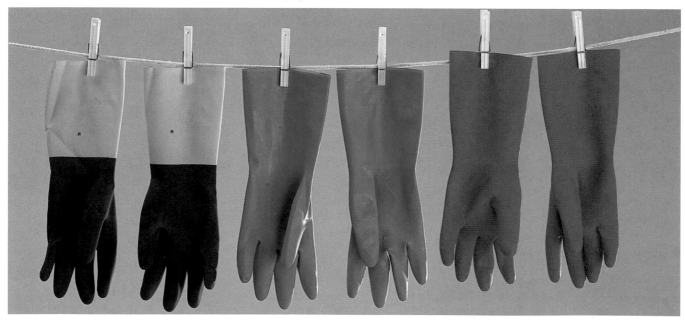

Gloves must be worn while dyeing.

WATER-SOLUBLE (WASHABLE) MARKERS. Transfer your designs onto fabric with these inexpensive children's markers. I don't recommend using pencil, because it may not come out of the final product. But these markers wash out during the dyeing and boiling process and leave nary a trace, although I try to use the lightest possible marker color just in case.

MISCELLANEOUS ITEMS. You may need some or all of the following items, depending on the projects you choose: clothespins, wax paper, wooden frame or canvas stretchers, masking tape, card stock or index cards, and cardboard. At some point, you may also need paper and/or fabric scissors, a ruler, a measuring stick or tape, and a pencil.

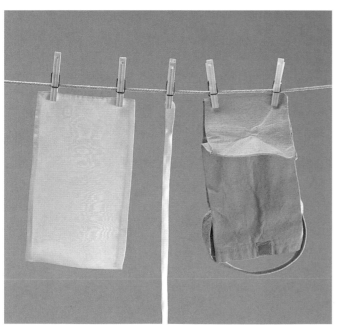

Fabric blanks

WHICH FABRICS WORK?

Batik offers you the freedom of creating your own personalized items that suit your taste and match your décor. You can successfully batik plant-based fibers such as cotton, rayon, linen, and hemp, as well as silk, which is a protein-based fiber. Bear in mind that synthetic fibers like polyester don't dye well, if at all, so look for natural fabrics like those listed above. (Although rayon is technically synthetic because it's manufactured, it's derived from cellulose and thus is considered plant based.) Synthetic fabrics can fool you, too, by appearing to take the dye, only to have it wash out later during the finishing process. If you like to sew, you can buy yardage of unbleached or white material and make your own pieces to dye.

You can let someone else do the sewing, though, as clothing and household blanks created specifically for wearable art are available from many mail order and/or Internet businesses. These are undyed garments such as blouses, shirts, and scarves, as well as home accessories such as pillow covers and table linens, some shown at left. Look for unbleached or white items at department or discount stores, too; the curtains on page 24 came from such a source.

If you plan on purchasing clothing blanks and haven't done much dyeing, I recommend going to a fabric store and buying just a small amount of a similar fabric to use for experimental swatches. You can play with the various wax tools to see how the material responds to that part of the process, and you can then use the swatches in the dyebath to determine when the fabric has reached a desired color. (Read more about this on page 17.) It's a small investment of time and money that will likely pay big dividends for you in the long run.

Finally, here's a simple way to tell whether a piece of fabric contains all natural fibers. Take a small piece of the material and burn it; synthetic fabrics burn quickly and melt, leaving a hard edge, while natural fibers burn slowly and leave a powdery ash.

THE BATIK PROCESS

Now that you have a basic understanding of the tools and materials for batik, are you ready to learn how? Here's a step-by-step guide to the process itself. Start with just a simple piece of fabric, like the one pictured in this section. Then, after you've read about this simplified technique, you'll find more than 20 projects to hone your skills.

Preparing the Fabric

The first step is easy: You simply wash and dry the fabric. You'll also preshrink the fabric in this step, which is important to do before you decorate the cloth. When you're handling the prepared fabric, make sure your hands are clean and don't iron the material unless absolutely necessary—anything you do to the fabric increases the chance that some substance may come in contact with it and act as a resist.

Applying the Wax

Melt the wax until it's liquid. With an electric skillet, you can set the temperature and keep it constant; I usually set the thermostat at around 250°F (122°C). After you've done batik for a while, you'll immediately know when the wax is the right temperature, because it should penetrate the fabric and appear somewhat transparent. If it's not hot enough, it will look cloudy or opaque and will sit on top of the fabric, rather than soak in. If it's too hot, it will run. Spend a little time experimenting with the wax before you begin in earnest. Practice until you get the hang of it.

Several factors come into play when you're trying to determine the right temperature for the hot wax. The properties of the fabric itself are important, because the thickness and density of weave can require you to adjust the temperature. For example, for the floorcloth project on page 65, I had to increase the temperature so the wax flowed properly into the heavy canvas cloth. If the wax doesn't appear to be soaking into the fabric, raise the temperature a few degrees. By contrast, you'll find that some fabrics, like silk and linen, take the wax readily.

While you're learning about the wax, you can also work with the various tools. In my opinion, the proper way to hold the tjanting is the way that's best for you. Experiment on some fabric scraps until you're comfortable with this tool. Draw lots of lines and squiggles to familiarize yourself with its qualities. Tjantings are inexpensive,

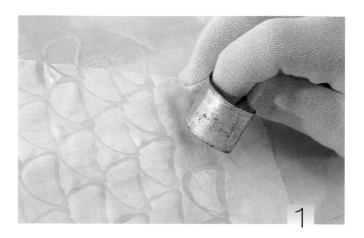

so you'll probably want to buy a couple with different size spouts for your projects.

If you're using stamps of any kind, you need to remove the excess wax before you move across the fabric you're decorating. You can either gently fling the wax off into the container with a slight flick of the wrist, or scrape off the excess on the side of the skillet. The methods produce different results; if you scrape off the wax, you'll have more color bleed through the wax impressions. The scarf project on page 32 illustrates more about these different techniques.

Use a piece of card stock or similar material to catch any drips from the tool as you move over the fabric. Press the stamp gently and firmly into place on the garment, as in photo 1. Continue as desired, dipping the stamp back into the wax before each new impression.

All of the tools should be heated in the wax for a few moments before you begin to work. You'll want the level of wax a little higher when you're using the tjanting tool as opposed to a stamping tool, because you need to be able to dip the bowl into the wax. The great thing is that you can leave the wax to solidify in the skillet until your next batik session; just cover it to keep away dust and dirt.

If you don't want the wax to penetrate through all the layers of a garment, use wax paper as a barrier underneath the layer being stamped. Change the paper as needed. Specific design techniques will be described in the project instructions, beginning on page 22.

Whoops! If you make a mistake when you're waxing, don't sweat it too much. Slight variations in the density of design or the application of color are part of handicraft, and a little drip of wax won't spoil the piece. Try to incorporate any mistakes into the design rather than attempting to fix them. It's difficult to stamp over a design again, for example, and the only way to effectively remove errant wax is to boil the fabric and start over again.

Dyeing the Fabric

After you've created a marvelous design on the surface of the fabric, it's time to bring it to life with color. Most of these projects are created by immersion dyeing, also called vat dyeing, in which the entire piece is submerged in a dyebath.

MIXING THE DYE

First, you've got to mix the dye. But, how much dye, how much water, and how long? There are some variables involved in deriving the formula to create just the right shade. For advice on this step, see How Much Water? How Much Dye? at right.

Once you've determined the proportions of each ingredient in the dyebath, but before you begin to mix, put on your rubber gloves, because you should avoid direct skin contact with the dye. Wear a mask to avoid breathing in the dye powder. Now, begin by mixing the dye with warm water in a small jar (photo 2). Shake vigorously to blend (photo 3). Next, add the dye to the tub

HOW MUCH WATER? HOW MUCH DYE?

This is perhaps the trickiest part of the entire process—how to mix the dye and achieve the result you want. Recommendations about mixing vary, and some of them are awfully confusing, frankly; most are based on the weight of the item being dyed. Do you have a scale that weighs a silk bag accurately? I sure don't.

So, I took all the information into account but used my own easy method, based on common sense instead of the ratio of fiber weight to water. (Just in case you want to know, the general figure is about 1 pound [454 g] of dry fabric to 3 gallons [11.4 L] of water.) I've provided dye formulas for each project, but the kind of dye you use, your desired color intensity, and the type of fabric you're dyeing are all factors in the process, too. (Remember the fabric swatches on page 12?) Use the figures in the projects as guidelines, and take notes while you work so you can re-create a favorite color or effect.

Here's how to mix the dye.

■ Take a look at the item you're batiking, and decide on the container you'll use for dyeing, one that will allow the item to remain as flat as possible when it's immersed in the mixture.

■ Add water to the tub with a pitcher, and keep track of how much you've used.

■ For every gallon (3.8 L) of water you've added, use about 1 cup (344 g) of salt. Add half the amount of washing soda as you do salt.

■ Add from 1 to 2 teaspoons (3 to 6 g) of dye for each gallon of water.

The dye amount is very general, because a dark color like navy can require as much as 4 tablespoons (36 g) per gallon of water. You'll need to experiment with the dyes a little to get the shades you want, but once you've dyed your first article or two, you'll get the hang of it. And they will be beautiful!

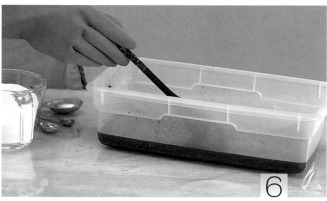

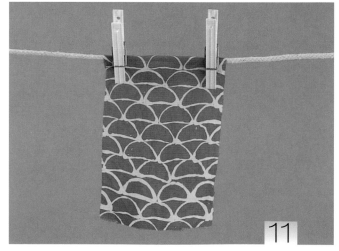

filled with lukewarm water and stir (photo 4). Add salt and stir (photo 5). Lastly, add the soda and yes, stir again (photo 6). All of the ingredients must be dissolved and mixed properly, or you may have spots from the undissolved dye.

IMMERSING THE FABRIC

After you've added the soda, you should begin to work immediately, because the dye is now active. It will be effective for only a couple of hours, after which time it begins to lose its potency and ability to dye. (This is a chemical reaction, remember.) Add the fabric (photo 7), and make sure that it's floating freely and isn't bunched or stuffed into the container. It should lie as flat as possible, but a large piece may have some gentle folds. That's why it's extremely important to manipulate it every couple of minutes (photo 8), moving it around so the dye affects the piece equally. The general rule is to leave pieces in the dye for about 30 minutes, but this can vary depending on the color saturation you want.

To check the progress of your work, toss in little scraps of fabric when you begin the dyeing step; pull them out every 10 minutes or so; rinse them; and hold them up to a light source to check the color. This last step is important, because the fabric will appear darker when it's wet, and the light helps you gauge what the shade will look like when the fabric is dry. Remove the piece when you're happy with the color and rinse it in cold water to remove all the dye.

If you've read about batik before, you may remember that the step just described is different from most other instructions. While some directions will have you submerge the fabric in the dye first, leave it for some time, remove it, add the soda, and then immerse the fabric once again, I've found that it isn't necessary to do that. All the ingredients can be added to the dyebath before the fabric is dipped—it's much easier and a lot less messy.

One important thing to note is that the chemical reaction of the dye begins to break down the wax after a couple of hours, causing erosion of the wax. Occasionally, you may need to leave a piece in for some time to achieve the color you want, particularly if it's a dark shade. To avoid degrading the wax, try adding a little black to your dye to darken it and reduce the necessary immersion time.

Be patient when you're learning, because acquiring a new skill takes some time and experimentation. The end result will be very rewarding and you'll have an awful lot of fun concocting your own colors. It's nothing less than modern-day wizardry!

Removing the Wax

There are two ways to remove the wax; I primarily used the boiling method. Before you use either, though, be sure to rinse the batiked item to remove the last traces of dye. Use lukewarm water. Be advised that fabrics dyed dark colors must be thoroughly rinsed, because so much dye has been used to create the deep shade.

BOILING

Here's another variation on the traditional process. Most sources will tell you to "boil" the fabric to remove the wax, and they'll warn you not to "boil" silk. I use a technique of wax removal that isn't really boiling, although I'll call it that in the instructions that follow. It works just fine on silk, too. For projects like the ones in this book, you can simply pour boiling water over the pieces and let the wax dissolve—*it's not necessary to actually boil the fabric itself.*

After the batiked article has been rinsed, place it in another tub on your work surface. Pour boiling water over the piece (photo 9), and then agitate it for about three minutes. Rinse it in cold water. (Use your collection of tubs for these steps.) If you still see wax on the surface, or the fabric seems stiff, boil it again, this time with a squirt of dishwashing detergent (photo 10).

Remember: When I use the term boil, I mean pour boiling water over the item—don't literally boil it.

All wastewater containing wax should be disposed of safely. Don't pour it down your drain, because it will solidify and eventually clog your pipes. The dyes, however, can be safely discharged in the drain.

IRONING

Here's an alternative to boiling; you can iron out all the wax into absorbent paper after your batik has air dried. This process is demonstrated in the slipcover project on page 42; place paper under and above the piece to be ironed and press. Replace the paper as needed while you're ironing. This method produces a characteristic "halo" formed by wax residue left in the fabric. But this halo effect doesn't appeal to all. To remedy this problem, wax and dye the piece, then hang to air dry. Next, wax over the entire piece before ironing it out.

Finishing the Process

After the wax has been removed, all you have to do is to wash and dry the piece (photo 11). You've made your first batik!

Applying the design in preparation for overdyeing

Painting with dye

Additional Techniques

Now that you understand the basic batik process, there are a couple of more advanced ideas you'll encounter in the book.

OVERDYEING

Overdyeing, or dyeing an item more than one time, is used to create multicolor designs. Because this book focuses on easy, contemporary applications of batik, you won't find any elaborate overdyed projects with multiple colors. But several of the projects do use this technique to create simple overdyed items, like the shoes on page 46 or the linens on page 59.

The basic premise behind adding color in batik is that you start with the lightest color and work your way to the darkest, blocking with wax everything you don't want dyed with that color or any of the successive colors. You have to consider the effects of combining color, too, because if you have a first layer of color that's yellow, and add a second of blue, you'll end up with a background of green. The projects included here use simple overdyeing methods. A blank article is merely dyed a solid color, then waxed with a design and dyed again, sometimes even the same color, just to produce a subtle variation in the final design. Each project that uses this technique will have complete instructions. The most important thing to remember is that you can only apply wax to fabric that's completely dry, so don't be tempted to rush through an overdyed project.

PAINTING WITH DYE

A couple of projects in the book involve painting the dye instead of, or in addition to, vat dyeing. This is a relatively simple process, explained in the project instructions, but you may note one thing that's a little scary when you do this. The dye can pool on top of the wax, but it still won't penetrate the resist if it's been applied properly. (See this effect below.) Remember to check the back of the fabric for dye saturation if you're creating a project that involves painting.

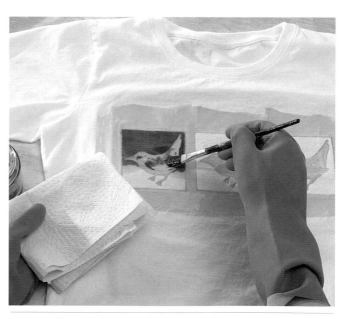

Dye pooling on the wax during painting

Additional Considerations

You're just about ready to starting batiking. Here are just a few last tips to help you get started in your new craft.

USING THE DESIGNS

This book is all about being creative with design and color. One wonderful thing about that is the motifs can be transferred to just about any project. Like the dog bed, but don't have a dog? Wouldn't that design make great curtains, too? Use these ideas to satisfy your own artistic vision. I've given you all the specifics about each project, so it will be easy to take a design from one project and use it on another.

CREATING A WORKPLACE

With my simple methods, you can easily set up a temporary batik workshop in your home. You'll need access to running water, electrical outlets, a stove, and a washer and dryer. Make sure you have adequate ventilation, as the hot wax will give off fumes.

In a perfect world, you could work outside. But using a series of tubs allows you to work inside and contain the dye and water. The tubs are easy to clean, too, especially if you have easy access to a hose. I dye in one tub, use a different one for rinsing, then perhaps a third one for the boiling step.

Your actual work surface should be level and have enough space to hold several tubs. I strongly urge you to

WHAT DO THE SYMBOLS MEAN?

When you're purchasing dyes, be aware of any special markings or symbols on the container; they probably mean you need more than the normal amount of dye to reach a medium shade. They may also indicate that you need to add more than the usual amount of salt. For instance, the navy and blue dyes I used required four times the normal amount of dye, and the black needed twice the salt. Inquire about this before you buy, and look to your craft store for advice about dyeing.

get some plastic sheeting and cover your working surface, because you'll probably get some drips of both wax and dye while you're batiking. The project shown below required some additional heavy plastic sheeting to protect the work table, in addition to the clear plastic I usually use. Yes, it can be a little messy. But because fiber-reactive dye reacts only to natural substances, it cleans up pretty easily and doesn't absorb into surfaces like tile.

Work on a protected surface.

WHAT DO I NEED?

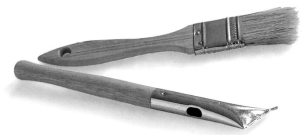

*B*ecause batik has several different phases of production, you'll need to have a variety of tools and materials on hand. Since many of the projects use the same items, I've compiled a master list of materials. Gather these supplies and keep them on hand. You won't need every tool or material for every project, of course. In each set of project instructions, I'll refer to the following as essential supplies:

For waxing:	For dyeing:
Electric skillet (or suitable alternative)	Tubs (a variety of sizes)
Wax	Dye
Tjanting	Soda
Brushes	Salt
Stamps (cookie cutters, spools, dowels, etc.)	Measuring tools (spoons, cups, pitchers)
Fabric gloves	Wooden spoons or tongs
Clothespins	Jars with tight-fitting lids
Index cards, card stock, or cardboard	Rubber gloves
Masking tape	Artist's brushes
Wax paper	Dishwashing detergent
Water-soluble markers	Laundry detergent

While I've noted the exact tool that I used for each stamping project, it's not absolutely necessary that you use one that's the same size. I give you permission to alter the designs! And, you'll also see that the fiber content of the items used in each project is listed in the materials list, too, for your information. But remember that you're free to experiment with different fabrics.

Working Safely

Exercise good judgment when you're working, and you'll have an enjoyable and creative day of batiking. Here's a checklist:

DO

Watch the temperature of the wax; wax is flammable. If it starts to smoke or boil, it's too hot. Extinguish a wax fire by smothering; don't use water under any circumstance.

Keep hot wax off your skin.

Wear a mask while you're mixing dye so you don't inhale the powder.

Keep the dyes away from food.

Work in an area that's well ventilated.

Dispose of wastewater safely.

DON'T

Forget to enjoy your new craft and make something fabulous! Gather up your supplies, let your creativity flow, and get started.

Lunch Bag

Spice up your lunchtime with this simple decorated bag—great for a picnic, too!

Essential supplies (page 20)

Scissors

Blank lunch bag (unbleached cotton canvas)

DYEBATH

3 Tbsp (27 g) warm red dye

2 c (688 g) salt

3/4 c (126 g) washing soda

2 gal (7.6 L) water

Immersion time: 30 minutes

Rinse, boil, wash, and dry.

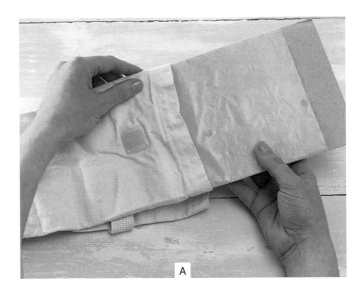

1 Cut a piece of cardboard to fit inside your bag, and wrap it with wax paper. Tape the wax paper in place on the back of the cardboard. Insert the cardboard into the bag (photo A). If your bag has pleated sides, like these, be sure the sides are under the cardboard so they are protected during the waxing step.

2 Use clothespins to secure the cardboard (photo B). Next, decide how many stamped motifs can fit on your bag, and determine the spacing. Mark the spacing if necessary.

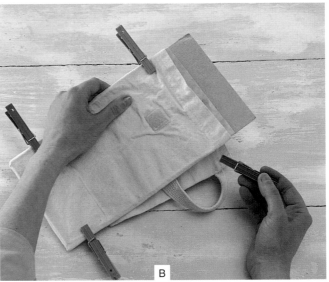

3 Let a wooden spool heat in the wax for a few moments, gently fling the excess, and begin stamping (photo C). Relocate the clothespins as necessary. When the front of the bag is covered with wax impressions, remove the cardboard and clothespins.

4 Mix the dyebath and finish as directed.

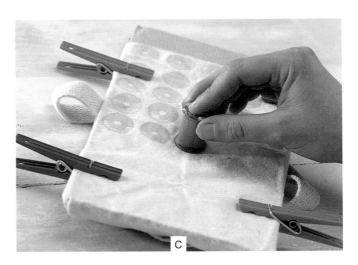

Café Curtains

Let these curtains flutter in a sunny window to accentuate their floral motif.

Essential supplies (page 20)

Undyed curtains (cotton)

Measuring tape

DYEBATH

3 Tbsp (27 g) dark green dye

2 tsp (6 g) yellow dye

6 c (2064 g) salt

1 1/2 c (252 g) washing soda

9 gal (34.2 L) water

Immersion time: 30 minutes

Rinse, boil, wash, and dry.

VARIATION

THOUGH IT'S EASY TO FIND UNDYED COTTON CURTAINS, YOU COULD CERTAINLY MAKE YOUR OWN, TOO.

1 Measure the curtains to determine the spacing of your floral pattern. Mark a spot for each row of flowers, if necessary, using a water-soluble marker. To prepare to batik, place wax paper underneath the curtains on your work surface.

2 You'll build this design by starting with the central dots, and then adding the petals. Use a 3/8-inch (9.5 mm) wooden dowel to make rows of dots, using a card underneath as you move the waxed dowel across the curtains (photo A).

3 When you've finished the rows of dots, take a heart-shaped cookie cutter as your next tool. Heat the cookie cutter in the wax for a few moments. Wear a fabric glove to protect your hands from the heat, and stamp four petals around each central dot (photo B). You might find that it's easier to add all the petals in one direction first to minimize the manipulation of the warm stamp.

4 Turn the curtain over. Hold it down with one hand and carefully peel away the wax paper (photo C).

5 Make the dyebath and finish as directed.

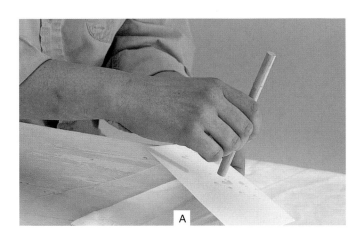

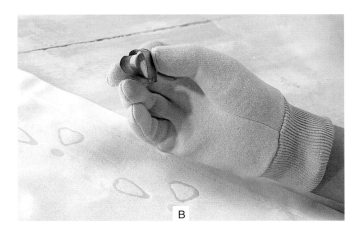

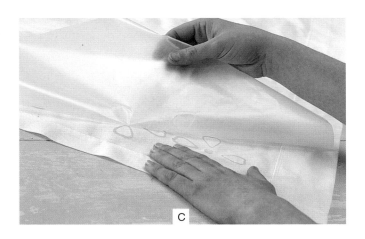

Envelope Pillows

These throw pillows have lines of batiked dots that form a clean, modern design.

MATERIALS

Essential supplies (page 20)

Blank pillow covers (bleached cotton duck)

Ruler

DYEBATH

3 Tbsp (27 g) brown dye

2 c (688 g) salt

1 c (344 g) washing soda

3 gal (11.4 L) water

Immersion time: 30 minutes

Rinse, boil, wash, and dry.

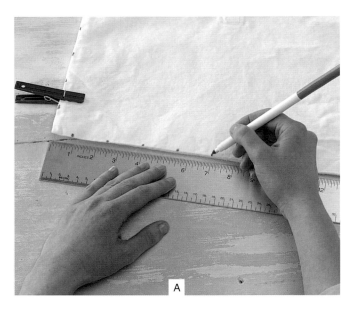

1 Place wax paper inside the pillow cover to prevent the wax from penetrating into the back of the pillow cover. Use clothespins to secure the wax paper, moving the clothespins as you work if necessary.

2 Measure and mark your design grid (photo A). This project features intersecting lines that form squares of 1^1/$_2$ inches (3.8 cm).

3 Place the ruler just to the side of your marks and use it as a guide to keep the stamped dots in a straight line. Stamp the design, using a dowel ^{3}/$_{16}$ inch (5 mm) in diameter (photo B). Remember to catch the drips with a card or similar tool.

4 Carefully remove the wax paper when you're finished stamping. Gently pull the front of the pillow cover away from the paper while you slide the wax paper out (photo C).

5 Mix the dyebath and finish as directed; this formula dyes two pillow covers.

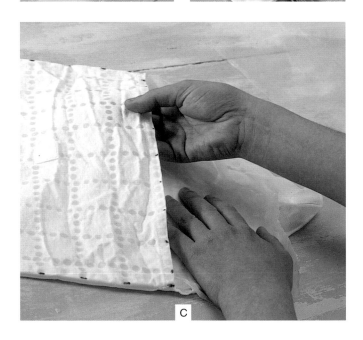

Bathing Suit

Use the tjanting and a brush to decorate this swimsuit with a jaunty hibiscus to make it absolutely perfect for an island getaway.

Essential supplies (page 20)
Blank swimsuit (cotton/lycra)
Template (page 76)
Pencil
Paper
Scissors

DYEBATH

2 Tbsp (18 g) fuchsia dye
2 c (688 g) salt
1 c (168 g) washing soda
3 gal (11.4 L) water
Immersion time: 12 minutes
Rinse, boil, wash, and dry.

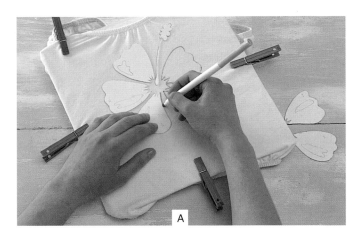

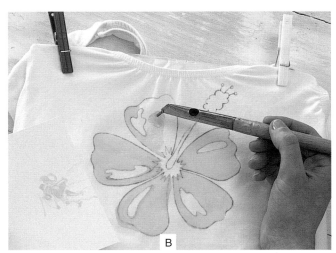

1 Cover a piece of cardboard with wax paper and secure it with tape. Stretch and pin the swimsuit around it. Be sure that the area to be waxed is centered on the cardboard.

2 Transfer the template onto paper, and then cut out the various pieces. Arrange them on the swimsuit and trace around each with a water-soluble marker (photo A). Freehand the inside shapes in the petals.

3 Use the tjanting to fill in the parts of the flower, starting with the outline and then filling in the interior of the design (photo B).

4 When you're finished waxing, carefully remove the swimsuit from the cardboard and hold it up to a light source. Look through the wrong side of the fabric and check to see if any light shows through the design. If you need to fill in any of the flower with more wax, use a brush to wax from the wrong side.

5 Prepare the dye bath and finish as directed. Manipulate the bathing suit well in the dyebath (photo C).

Adorned Ribbons

Although these ribbons will grace any gift, they're versatile enough to make lovely hair accessories, too.

1 Cut the ribbons to your desired length(s). To protect your hands from the heated stamp in this project, clip a clothespin onto a pastry tip (photo A) and use the clothespin as a handle.

2 Dip the icing tip in the wax, fling gently, and stamp a solid circle of wax on the ribbon. Continue stamping without dipping the tip back in hot wax, until you're leaving just a ring of wax (photo B). Repeat to decorate the entire ribbon.

3 Use this technique to create a variety of patterns. Try running the circle off the edge and onto wax paper, or making a floral motif by surrounding a solid dot with circular ones. Note the different patterns (photo C).

4 Add the ribbons to the various dye baths as you make other projects, and gradually build a collection of them as you work. If you prefer to make a quantity that are all the same color, make sure your dye bath contains at least a gallon (3.8 L) of water, so you have enough water to manipulate the ribbons.

5 After dyeing, rinse, boil, wash, and hang to dry; the ribbons tend to fray and get caught in the dryer, so be sure to let them air dry (photo D).

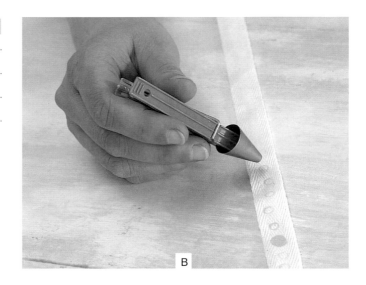

B

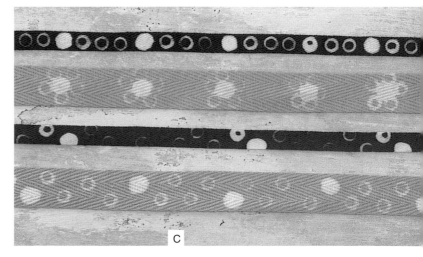

C

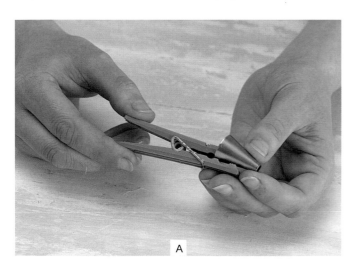

A

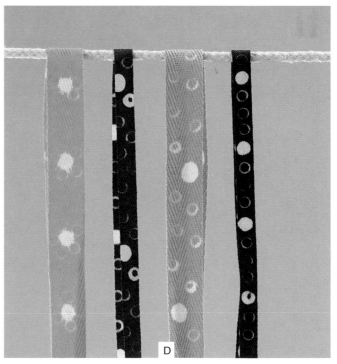

D

Silk Scarves

The height of sophistication, these exquisite scarves are created with a simple wooden block.

MATERIALS

Essential supplies (page 20)

Blank scarves (silk crêpe de Chine)

Measuring stick

DYEBATH

2 tsp (6 g) periwinkle dye

$1^1/_2$ c (516 g) salt

$^1/_2$ c (84 g) washing soda

2 gal (7.6 L) water

Immersion time: 30 minutes

Rinse, boil, wash, and dry.

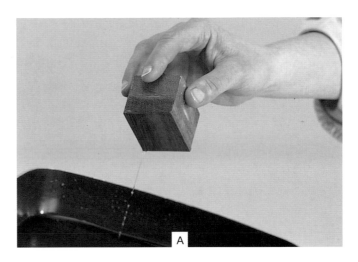

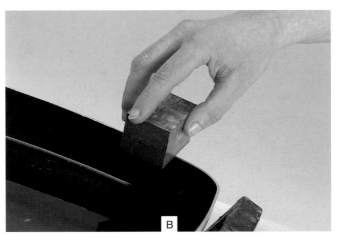

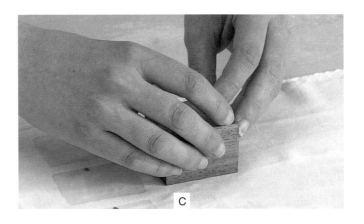

1 Measure the scarf and wooden block to determine the number of rectangles that will fit across the width of the scarf. Fold the scarf end to end, find and pinch the middle, and mark three dots to designate the starting point for your design. Place wax paper under the scarf.

2 To form predominantly solid white rectangles, fling the excess wax off the block before stamping (photo A). This effect is shown in the blue scarf, at the left in the photo on page 32.

3 For more color within the rectangles, scrape the block on the edge of the skillet before stamping (photo B). The chartreuse scarf at the right in the photo on page 32 demonstrates this effect.

4 Stamp the middle three rectangles, centering the edge of the block on the marks. Continue stamping down one side, having equal space between the rows (photo C). Leave a border.

5 Return to the middle of the scarf and stamp to the other end (photo D).

6 Turn the scarf over and hold it down as you carefully peel off the wax paper (photo E).

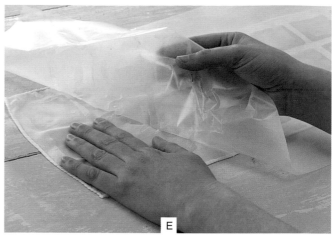

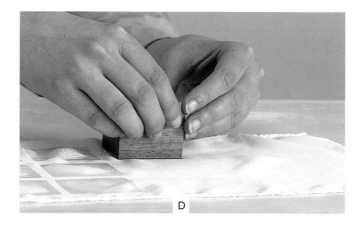

7 Make the dyebath for the blue scarf as indicated, and finish as directed. The chartreuse scarf was dyed in the same bath as the linens; the formula for that color appears on page 60.

Diamond Shirt

This clever pattern adds a classy touch to this shirt,
and once you get the design started, you merely follow the grid.

MATERIALS

Essential supplies (page 20)
Blank man's shirt (cotton)

DYEBATH

16 Tbsp (144 g) navy dye
4 c (1376 g) salt
2 c (336 g) washing soda
4 gal (15.2 L) water
Rinse, boil, wash, and dry.

1 Place wax paper underneath the placket of the shirt. Rotate a $^5/_{16}$-inch-square (8 mm) wooden dowel to use as a diamond-shaped stamp. Begin at the bottom of the placket on the outer edge, making half diamond shapes on the shirt by stamping off the edge of the fabric onto the wax paper (photo A). (Be sure to lightly fling the excess wax when stamping this project; don't scrape it off.) Leave equal space between each diamond, about $^3/_{16}$ inch (5 mm) between each shape.

2 Begin the second row next to the first row, offset one-half diamond (photo B). When you're done, the straight edges should be parallel with one another. Be aware of the space between the motifs and keep it equal, as best you can.

3 Continue stamping rows. When you reach the other side of the placket, fold the shirt around wax paper-covered cardboard and secure the shirt with clothespins. Stamp off the edge leaving just the half-diamond designs as on the first row (photo C).

4 Button up the shirt and visually line up the collar with the lines on the placket. Stamp the collar as you did the placket, folding the cloth around the cardboard and using a clothespin when needed (photo D).

5 Make the dyebath and finish as instructed. (Yes, it takes lots of dye for dark colors!) Be sure to manipulate the shirt well during the dyebath and rinse thoroughly.

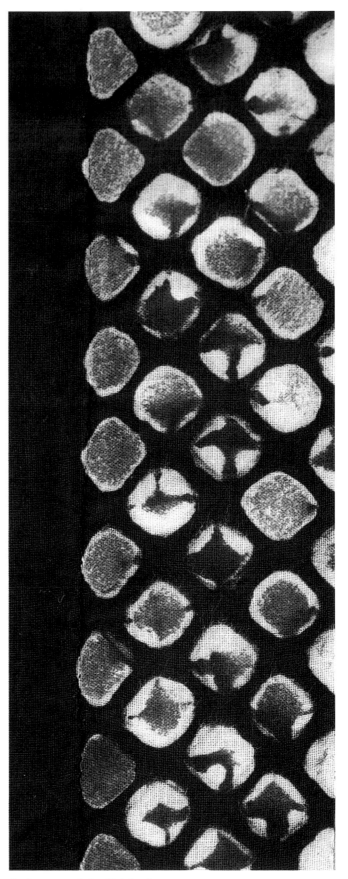

A close-up of the finished pattern

Phases of the Moon Dog Bed

Any pooch would love to snooze on this stylish bed, whose design recalls a moon calendar.

MATERIALS

Essential supplies (page 20)

Large blank pillow cover (bleached cotton duck)

Long measuring stick or measuring tape

Old blanket

DYEBATH

16 Tbsp (144 g) black dye

8 c (2752 g) salt

3 c (504 g) washing soda

4 gal (15.2 L) water

Immersion time: 30 minutes

Rinse, boil, wash, and dry. Add dog!

1 Fill the inside of the pillow cover with wax paper and clip it in place with clothespins. Using a measuring stick and a water-soluble marker, make a grid of 144 equidistant dots, 12 vertical by 12 horizontal (photo A).

2 Fold an old blanket and place it underneath the pillow cover, because it'll help you make good impressions in the heavy cotton duck. (Be sure to use an old blanket, just in case it winds up with a little wax on it.)

3 Use varying sizes of dowels or spools as tools; if you use a spool, fill in the bottom with putty, allow it to dry, and sand it smooth so you have a solid surface. Using a card to catch the drips, first stamp a row of 12 horizontal and 12 vertical dots with the largest diameter tool, centering the tool on the marks. Repeat this step with the same tool, stamping next to the first rows. Be sure you gently fling, not scrape, the excess wax before you stamp so you create the proper effect in this project.

4 Scale down to the next largest tool and stamp the horizontal and vertical rows next to previous ones;

you'll be stamping smaller and smaller rows as you move toward the unstamped corner of the cover (photo B). From this point forward, make only one row with each tool; this project features 11 tools altogether. To lessen the number of tools required, use each stamp for two rows, for example.

5 When you've finished stamping, remove the wax paper and clothespins.

6 Prepare the dyebath and complete as directed. Remember to rinse well. Photo C illustrates the effect in the finished piece.

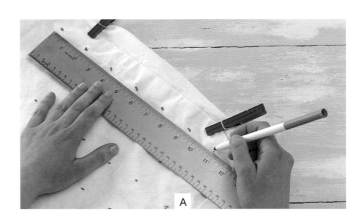

A

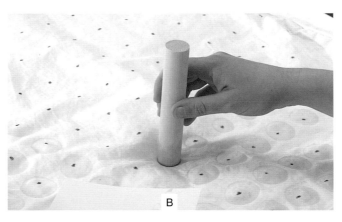

B

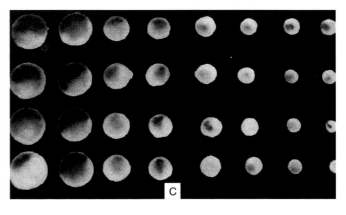

C

Starry Top

Create this cheerful constellation of stars by stamping with a set of graduated cookie cutters.

Essential supplies (page 20)

Blank top (rayon)

Star-shaped metal cookie cutters (in several sizes)

DYEBATH

2 tsp (6 g) pink dye

$1^1/_2$ c (516 g) salt

$^1/_2$ c (84 g) washing soda

3 gal (11.4 L) water

Immersion time: 30 minutes

Rinse, boil, wash, and dry.

A

D

B

E

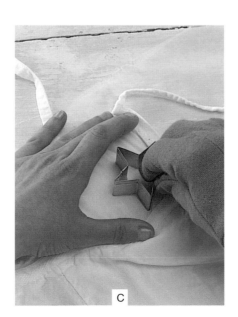

C

1 Let the cookie cutters warm up in the hot wax before you begin (photo A).

2 Place wax paper under the blank top. Wearing a fabric glove, dip the cookie cutter in the hot wax and gently fling away the excess (photo B). Be sure to use a card or similar material underneath as you move the cutter across the top to begin stamping.

3 Use your hands to manipulate the fabric so you have an even surface on which to stamp (photo C). Arrange the waxed impressions as you choose.

4 Continue stamping off the edge of the top. Then, stamp some small stars inside some of the larger stars (photo D). When your pattern is complete, remove the wax paper.

5 If your blank top has straps that tie, like the one in this project, untie any knots at the ends of the straps before the dyebath, because the knots will prevent the dye from saturating the fabric.

6 Prepare the dyebath and finish as directed. Be sure to keep moving the top to ensure even dyeing (photo E).

Striped Slipcovers

These elegant slipcovers exhibit the distinctive halo effect obtained by ironing out the wax.

MATERIALS

Essential supplies (page 20)

Cotton fabric

Long measuring stick

Fabric scissors

Iron

Paper towels or plain newsprint

Pins and pin cushion

Sewing machine

Thread (to match the dyed fabric)

DYEBATH

2 Tbsp (18 g) lapis blue dye

3 c (1032 g) salt

1 c (168 g) washing soda

4 gal (15.2 L) water

Immersion time: 20 minutes

Rinse. Hang the pieces to dry; don't put them in the dryer.

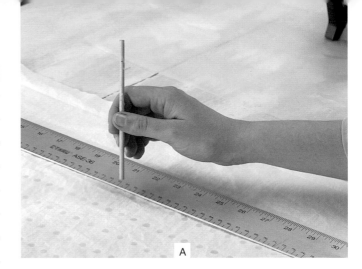

A

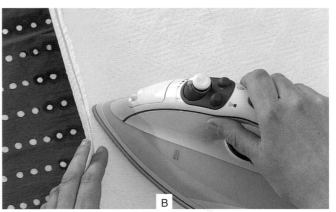

B

C

1 Measure the backs of the chairs that you wish to cover, and be sure to add a little extra for seam allowances as well as the thickness of the wood. Cut out two pieces of fabric per chair according to your measurements, one for the front and one for the back of the slipcover. In this project, only the front panel is decorated; the finished slipcover is $15^{1}/_{2}$ x $24^{1}/_{2}$ inches (39.4 x 62.2 cm).

2 Use the measuring stick to mark dots at $1^{1}/_{4}$-inch (3.2 cm) intervals along the top and bottom of the fabric. Be sure you don't use the markers where they will be visible on the fabric, because these pieces won't be boiled and thus the marker won't be removed.

3 Wax dots with a $^{3}/_{16}$-inch (5 mm) dowel, using the measuring stick as a visual guide. Follow a straight line from the top of the piece to the bottom, making a dot every $^{1}/_{2}$ inch (1.3 cm) or so (photo A). Remember to flick the wax off the dowel and use a card or similar tool underneath when working across the fabric.

4 Make the dyebath as indicated.

5 To remove the wax and create the halo effect, use an iron. Lay absorbent paper (paper towels or plain newsprint) both under and on top of the fabric and press, changing the paper as needed (photo B).

6 Hem the bottoms of the front and back pieces. Place the right sides of the panels together and stitch the seams (photo C) .

Chiffon Sarong

This graceful garment can be dressed down for a day at the beach or dressed up for a night on the town.

Essential supplies (page 20)

Blank sarong (silk chiffon)

Wooden frame or canvas stretchers

Silk pins (from a craft store)

DYEBATH 1

2 Tbsp (18 g) fuchsia dye

1 Tbsp (9 g) violet dye

1 Tbsp (9 g) navy dye

$1^1/_2$ c (516 g) salt

$^3/_4$ c (126 g) soda

3 gal (11.4 L) water

Immersion time: 1 hour

Rinse and dry.

DYEBATH 2

16 Tbsp (144 g) navy dye

3 c (1032 g) salt

$1^1/_2$ c (252 g) washing soda

3 gal (11.4 L) water

Immersion time: $3^1/_2$ hours

Rinse, boil, wash, and dry.

1 You'll dye the sarong first, then dye it a second time after you've added the surface design. Prepare the initial dye bath.

2 Stretch a section of the sarong on the wooden frame and secure it with silk pins (photo A). Stretch evenly, so the weave of the fabric is perpendicular to the frame.

3 Fill this section with freehand dragonflies, with a squiggle for a body, ovals for the wings, and dots for the eyes. When you've completed that segment, remove the pins and repeat as necessary, until you've filled the entire sarong with dragonflies (photo B).

4 Mix a second dye bath for overdyeing.

5 Note the slight deterioration that occurred in the finished project during the long immersion time. The wax eroded somewhat, but this effect adds to the charm of this piece (photo C).

TIP

CHIFFON CLINGS TO ITSELF, SO GENTLY MANIPULATE IT WHILE DYEING. ALSO, BE CAREFUL WHEN YOU DYE A LARGE PIECE LIKE THIS, BECAUSE YOU'RE MORE LIKELY TO END UP WITH DYE ON YOUR ARMS, SINCE YOU HAVE TO PULL IT OUT OF THE DYEBATH A FAIR DISTANCE WHEN YOU'RE HANDLING IT.

A

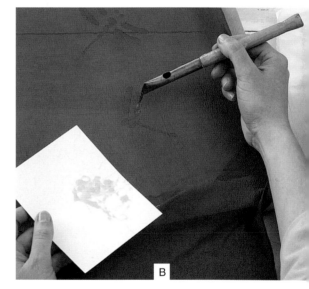

B

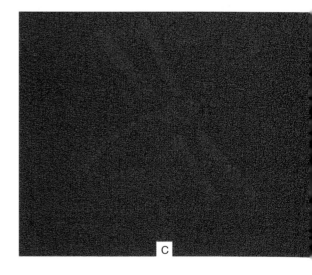

C

Fabric Shoes

*Imagination is the key to this fanciful footwear, because you can
create almost any design with found objects.*

MATERIALS

Essential supplies (page 20)

Blank shoes (cotton twill)

DYEBATH 1

3 Tbsp (27 g) turquoise dye

1 c (344 g) salt

$^{1}/_{2}$ c (84 g) washing soda

$1^{1}/_{2}$ gal (5.7 L) water

Immersion time: 20 minutes

Rinse and hang to dry.

DYEBATH 2

10 Tbsp (90 g) navy dye

$1^{1}/_{2}$ c (516 g) salt

$^{3}/_{4}$ c (126 g) washing soda

$1^{1}/_{2}$ gal (5.7 L) water

Immersion time: 30 minutes

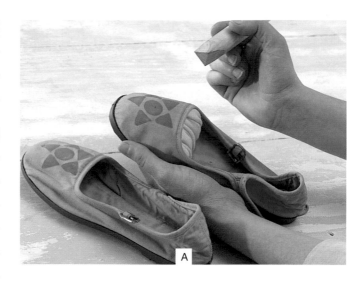

A

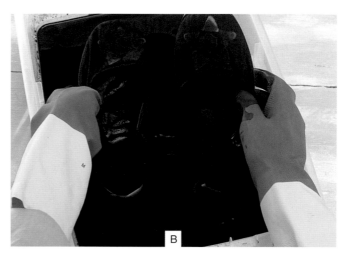

B

1 As you'll overdye these shoes, start by preparing the first dye bath. Don't put shoes with rubber soles in the dryer, though—they'll melt.

2 Prepare the shoes by folding a fabric glove and stuffing it into the toe, so you have a taut surface on which to work. Mark the center of the toe with a water-soluble marker, then stamp with a $^{3}/_{4}$-inch (1.9 cm) round dowel.

3 Now, switch to a triangle-shaped tool with $^{3}/_{4}$-inch (1.9 cm) sides and stamp around the center circle (photo A). (If you have difficulty finding a triangle-shaped tool, take a $^{7}/_{8}$-inch [2.2 cm] round dowel and chisel or sand the sides to make a stamp.)

4 Mix the second dyebath. Remember to manipulate the shoes often (photo B).

5 Rinse thoroughly to remove all the excess dye. Boil as needed (photo C). Air dry.

C

TIP

THE TURQUOISE DYE IN THIS RECIPE HAS TO BE MIXED WITH VERY HOT TAP WATER. BE SURE TO CHECK THE DYE YOU CHOOSE FOR ANY SUCH VARIATIONS; IF YOU'RE JUST LEARNING ABOUT DYES, ASK FOR ADVICE AT YOUR FAVORITE CRAFT STORE. SEE THE NOTE ABOUT DYES ON PAGE 19.

Paisley Pillow

*These luxurious pillows feature a subtle overdyed design created with a paisley stamp,
or tjap, made with simple tools.*

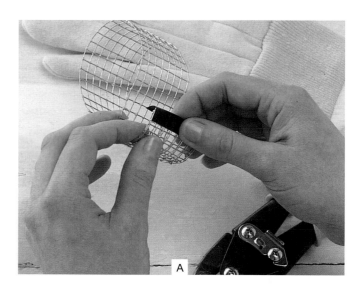

MATERIALS

Essential supplies (page 20)

Blank zippered pillow covers (Habotai silk)

1/4-inch (6 mm) hardware cloth

Tin snips or wire cutters

Electrical tape

DYEBATH 1

1 tsp (3 g) golden yellow dye

3/4 c (258 g) salt

1/4 c (42 g) washing soda

1 gal (3.8 L) water

Immersion time: 1 minute or less

Rinse and dry.

DYEBATH 2

2 tsp (6 g) golden yellow dye

1 1/2 c (516 g) salt

1/2 c (84 g) washing soda

2 gal (7.6 L) water

Immersion time: 30 minutes

Rinse, boil, wash, and dry.

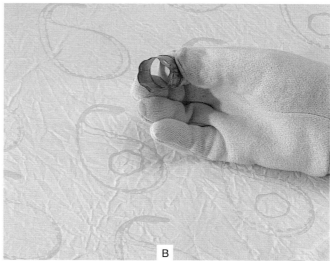

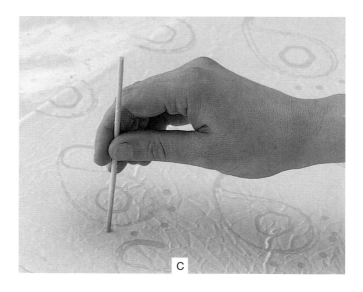

1 Make the dyebath for the initial dyeing. Note the brief immersion time.

2 Cover a piece of cardboard with wax paper and tape to secure the paper. Insert the cardboard into the pillow covers. You may need to flex or fold the cardboard to fit inside, but then flatten it out again after you've inserted it. Close the zipper. Place wax paper under the pillow.

3 Make the paisley tjap: Snip a length of hardware cloth, without leaving jagged edges, to your desired size. (The stamp in this project is approxi- mately 2 x 11 inches [5 x 27.9 cm].) Bend the strip of hardware cloth into a paisley shape and secure it with electrical tape (photo A).

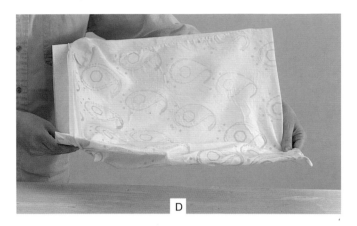

D

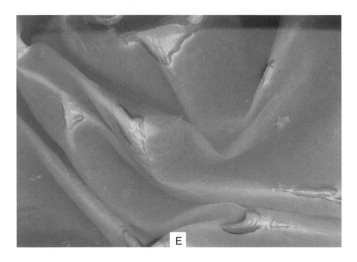

E

4 Stamp the paisleys in rows, offsetting the designs. Continue the design off all four edges, stamping onto the wax paper as needed. Stamp each paisley twice, making the second impression slightly off-register from the first. Wear a fabric glove when you use the metal cookie cutter to stamp inside each paisley (photo B, page 49).

5 Next, use a narrow dowel or the end of a brush to make five small dots around the head of the paisley, following the curve of the motif (photo C, page 49).

6 When you've completed the design, open the zipper, gently loosen the fabric from the cardboard, and carefully remove it (photo D).

7 Make the second dyebath, immerse as shown, and finish as indicated (photo E). Repeat steps 1 through 7 for as many pillows as desired.

Wine Gift Bag

*A special libation deserves a special presentation…a silk bag embellished with
a dramatic spiral and sparkling beads suits the mood.*

MATERIALS

Essential supplies (page 20)

Blank bag and tie (Habotai silk)

Template (page 75)

Card stock

Pencil

Craft knife

Cutting mat

Beads, beading silk, and needle (optional)

DYEBATH 1

1 tsp (3 g) plum dye

$^1/_2$ c (172 g) salt

$^1/_4$ c (42 g) washing soda

1 gal (3.8 L) water

Immersion time: 2 minutes

Rinse and dry.

DYEBATH 2

3 Tbsp (27 g) red wine dye

$^1/_4$ tsp (750 mg) black dye

1 c (344 g) salt

$^1/_2$ c (84 g) washing soda

1 gal (3.8 L) water

Immersion time: 1 hour.

Rinse, boil, wash, and dry.

1 Begin by dyeing the bag and the tie. Prepare the first dyebath and finish as instructed.

2 Set the tie aside, as it won't be dyed again. Cover a piece of cardboard with wax paper and secure it with tape; insert it inside the bag. Transfer the template onto card stock and use the craft knife to cut out a stencil (photo A).

3 Place the stencil on the bag and trace it with a water-soluble marker (photo B). Remove the stencil.

4 Use the tjanting to cover the marker line with wax (photo C). Remove the cardboard.

5 Make a second dyebath and complete as directed.

6 Add bead embellishments as desired.

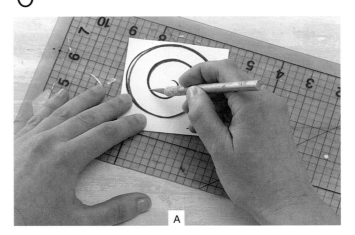

A

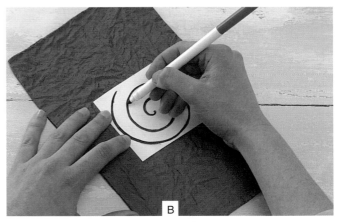

B

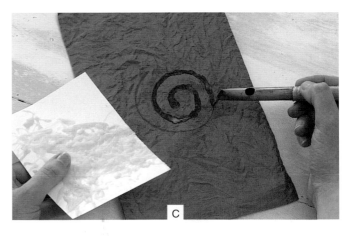

C

Twining Table Runner

Add a nature-inspired motif to a beautiful piece of linen for a memorable accessory.

Essential supplies (page 20)

Linen fabric (handkerchief weight)

Measuring tape

Fabric scissors

100 percent cotton thread

Sewing machine

DYEBATH 1

1 Tbsp (9 g) dark green dye

$3/4$ tsp (2 g) yellow dye

$1^1/2$ c (516 g) salt

$1/2$ c (84 g) washing soda

3 gal (11.4 L) water

Immersion time: 5 minutes

Rinse and dry the fabric.

DYEBATH 2

4 Tbsp (36 g) dark green dye

$3/4$ tsp (2 g) yellow dye

2 c (688 g) salt

1 c (168 g) washing soda

3 gal (11.4 L) water

Immersion time: 35 minutes

Rinse, boil, wash, and dry.

TIP

BE SURE TO USE PURE COTTON THREAD TO HEM THE TABLE RUNNER, BECAUSE A SYNTHETIC BLEND WON'T ABSORB THE DYE.

1 To begin, determine the size of your table runner and cut the fabric accordingly. Mix the initial dyebath and finish as directed.

2 Make a simple machine hem along the edges of the dyed table runner (photo A).

3 Place wax paper beneath the runner. Plan the spacing of the design and use a water-soluble marker to first draw the vines on the table runner (photo B).

4 Use the tjanting to trace your vines and fill in the leaves (photo C). Remember to hold a card under the tjanting when moving across the fabric. Add a triangle of dots between each segment of vines. Peel off the wax paper when you're done.

5 Make the second dyebath and finish as directed.

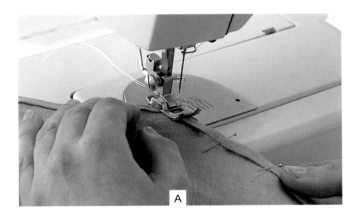

A

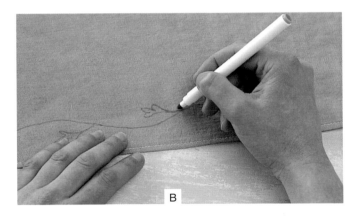

B

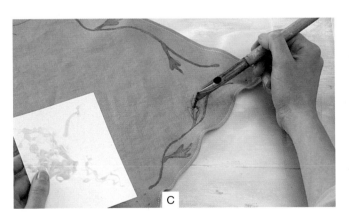

C

Triptych Wall Hanging

This lovely grouping of panels, reminiscent of an autumn day, is created by waxing the background and dyeing the leaves.

MATERIALS

Essential supplies (page 20)

Linen fabric (handkerchief weight)

Measuring tape

Fabric scissors

Template (page 75)

DYEBATH

1 tsp (3 g) beige dye

$^1\!/_2$ c (172 g) salt

$^1\!/_8$ c (21 g) washing soda

$1^1\!/_2$ gal (5.7 L) water

Immersion time: 5 minutes

Rinse and hang to dry.

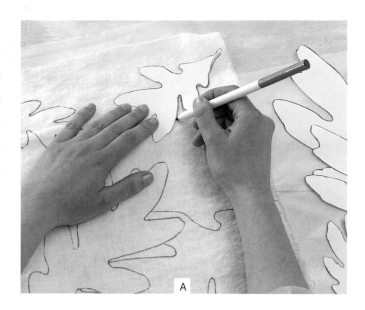

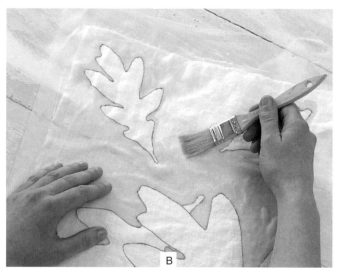

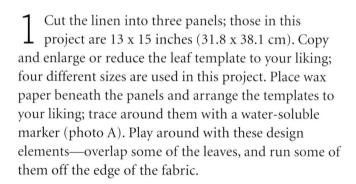

1 Cut the linen into three panels; those in this project are 13 x 15 inches (31.8 x 38.1 cm). Copy and enlarge or reduce the leaf template to your liking; four different sizes are used in this project. Place wax paper beneath the panels and arrange the templates to your liking; trace around them with a water-soluble marker (photo A). Play around with these design elements—overlap some of the leaves, and run some of them off the edge of the fabric.

2 Use the tjanting to trace the outlines of the leaves; don't wax the outlines where two leaves overlap. Use a brush (photo B) to wax the background.

3 Carefully turn the panel over and peel away the wax paper. It's okay if you can't peel it all off from the waxed areas, but be sure none adheres to the unwaxed leaf shapes.

4 Hold the panel up to a light source to check for any missed spots; look through the back side (photo C). Wax over any spots from the back side, if necessary.

5 Choose a tub big enough for the panels to lie flat, and mix the first dyebath. Complete as directed.

6 Decide which leaves will be the lightest color and wax over them. If your design features overlapping leaves, decide which of the leaves will be on top and mark their outlines where they cross the bottom leaves. Then wax the leaves you've chosen to be the lighter of the two (photo D). Peel away the wax paper and check the waxing, as in step 4.

7 Prepare the second dyebath as in step 5, but immerse the panels for 30 minutes. Rinse and boil as necessary; this project may require several boils to remove all the wax. Wash and dry.

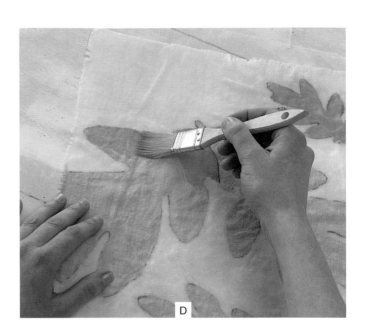

D

Gingham Linens

Enliven a traditional design with a jazzy color choice and create a distinctive look for your table.

DYEBATH

1¹/₂ Tbsp (14 g) chartreuse dye

4 c (1375 g) salt

1 c (168 g) washing soda

9 gal (34.2 L) water

Immersion time: 5 minutes

Rinse and hang to dry.

1 To batik the napkins, first measure the width of your desired border; dot at each corner with water-soluble marker. Place wax paper underneath the napkin. Dip a 1-inch (2.5 cm) square dowel in wax, scrape the excess on the edge of the skillet, and stamp along the edge of the border. Be sure to leave 1-inch (2.5 cm) spaces between the waxed impressions. Then, fill in the middle with wax squares (photo A).

2 To create the batiked border on the tablecloth, use the same technique as in step 1, but stamp the design around the edge of the tablecloth, making the rows 1 inch (2.5 cm) apart. Continue until the border is as wide as you want.

3 Mix the dye for the first dyebath (for both the tablecloth and napkins). They'll look like the photo B after they're dyed.

4 For the second waxing, stamp between the first waxed squares so the second stamps are adjacent to the first squares, both vertically and horizontally (photo C). Repeat for each napkin and the tablecloth. Remove the wax paper when you've completed the second waxing.

5 Prepare the second dyebath with the same formula as the first, but immerse the items for 30 minutes. Rinse and boil as necessary. (These were boiled three times.) Wash and dry; your linens will look like this when completed (photo D).

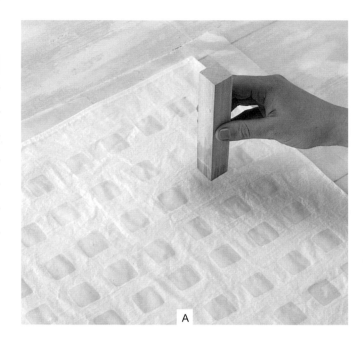

A

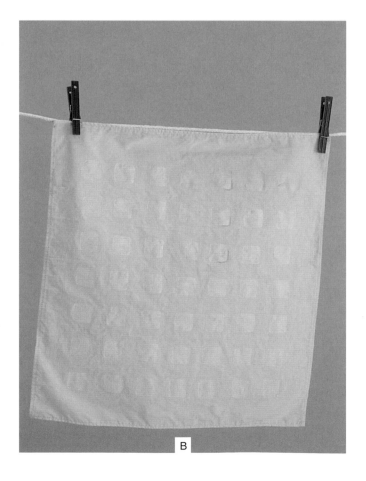

B

C

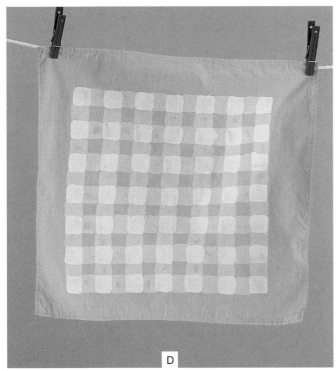

D

TIP

BE SURE TO USE A LARGE DYE TUB FOR THIS PROJECT. AFTER THE SECOND WAXING, THE TABLECLOTH IS PRETTY MUCH COVERED WITH WAX AND FOLDING IT TO FIT IN A SMALL TUB WOULD CRACK THE WAX.

ALTERNATIVE

IF YOU HAVE TROUBLE FINDING UNDYED LINENS, IT'S VERY SIMPLE TO MAKE YOUR OWN. CUT COTTON FABRIC TO YOUR DESIRED DIMENSIONS AND ADD A QUICK MACHINE HEM.

Glowing Sconce

This pattern, based on a Balinese design, will infuse any room with subtle beauty.

MATERIALS

Essential supplies (page 20)

Hemp/silk blend fabric

Ruler or measuring tape

Fabric scissors

Tin snips or wire cutters

$1/4$-inch (6 mm) hardware cloth

Clear liquid decoupage medium (brush optional)

Silver craft wire

DYEBATH 1

4 tsp (12 g) rust orange dye

$1^1/_2$ c (516 g) salt

$1/_2$ c (84 g) washing soda

2 gal (7.6 L) water

Immersion time: 10 minutes

Rinse and dry the fabric.

DYEBATH 2

3 Tbsp (27 g) dark brown dye

1 c (344 g) salt

$1/_2$ c (84 g) washing soda

$1^1/_2$ gal (5.7 L) water

Immersion time: 35 minutes

Rinse, boil, wash, and dry.

1 Cut the fabric to your desired size (this piece was 8 x 15¹/₄ inches [20.3 x 38.7 cm]). Then, dye the fabric and finish as directed for the first dyebath.

2 Place wax paper over your work surface. Use a water-soluble marker and ruler to draw the double-line grid on the fabric. Use a cookie cutter to stamp inside each square formed by the grid of lines (photo A).

3 Use a ³/₈-inch (9.5 mm) square dowel to stamp inside each square (photo B).

4 Switch to the tjanting and trace over the lines you drew in step 2. When you are waxing the longer lines, you'll need to stop halfway and reheat and refill the tjanting. Then, start again where you stopped (photo C). Peel off the wax paper when you've finished the design.

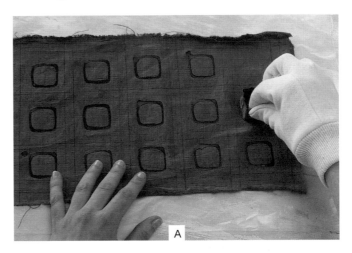

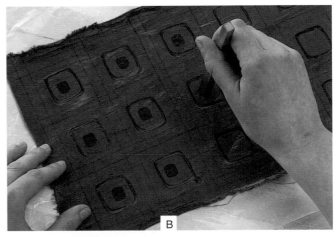

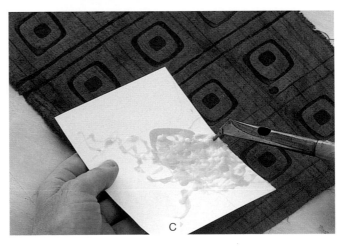

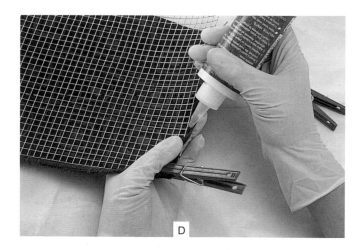

D

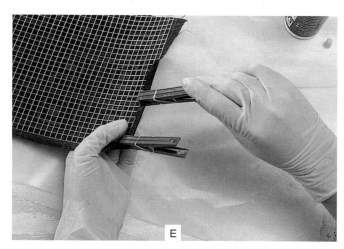

E

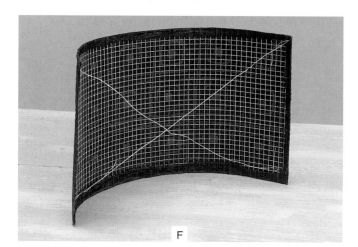

F

5 Now, make the second dye bath and finish as directed.

6 Use tin snips or wire cutters to cut the hardware cloth so it's slightly smaller than your fabric, about $3/8$ inch (9.5 mm) all around; here, the hardware cloth is $7^1/4$ x $14^1/2$ inches (18.4 x 36.8 cm). Wear protective gloves when you cut the hardware cloth, as the edges are very sharp. Clip the wire cleanly, so it isn't jagged. If necessary, gently curve the hardware cloth into the proper shape.

7 Wear disposable latex gloves to apply the decoupage medium along the edges of the cloth, using your fingers or a brush to push it into the fabric (photo D). Use clothespins to hold the fabric to the metal cloth while it's drying, affixing them as you work.

8 Fold the corners as if you were covering a book, (photo E). Use your fingers or a brush to cover the remainder of the fabric with decoupage medium.

9 To finish, attach 2 lengths of wire across the back from corner to corner (photo F). Pull the wires tight enough to form the shape of your sconce. Let it dry fully before mounting; use the wire to hang the sconce.

TIP

EXPERIMENT WITH THIS BASIC IDEA: IF YOU DON'T HAVE AN EXISTING FIXTURE ON WHICH TO HANG THE SCONCE, GET SOME BATTERY-OPERATED HOLIDAY LIGHTS AND TWIST THEM AROUND THE WIRE FOR ILLUMINATION. THEN, MOUNT THE SCONCE ON THE WALL.

Fantastic Floorcloth

Use lime green dye to add some pizzazz to this floorcloth.

MATERIALS

Essential supplies (page 20)

Heavy cotton canvas (unbleached)

Measuring stick

Fabric scissors

Sewing machine

100 percent cotton thread

Template (page 74)

Heavy paper or cardboard

Pencil

Scissors

Heavy plastic sheeting

DYEBATH 1

2 Tbsp (18 g) turquoise dye

3 c (1032 g) salt

1 c (168 g) washing soda

4 gal (15.2 L) water

Immersion time: 20 minutes

Rinse and hang to dry.

DYEBATH 2

1 Tbsp (9 g) lime green dye

2 Tbsp (43 g) salt

1 Tbsp (12 g) soda

$^1/_2$ c (120 mL) water

Leave the dye to sit for one hour, then rinse and hang to dry.

DYEBATH 3

3 Tbsp (27 g) forest green dye

2 Tbsp (43 g) salt

1 Tbsp (12 g) washing soda

1 c (240 mL) water

1 Cut the canvas to your desired dimensions and hem; this project measures 20 x 33 inches (50.8 x 83.8 cm). Prepare the first dyebath and dye the entire piece. It's important to let this heavy canvas drip dry, because it tends to fold and crease in the washer and/or dryer, leading to dye lines in these areas.

2 Measure and mark the placement of the design according to the size of your floorcloth, if necessary, remembering to leave space for the motif borders and margins. Transfer the template onto paper or cardboard and cut it out. Use a water-soluble marker to trace the template onto the cloth.

3 In a jar, mix the second dyebath. Use a $^1/_2$-inch (1.3 cm) brush to paint dye around the insides of the template outlines (photo A). Paint quickly, because the dye starts to weaken as soon as it is mixed. If you're making a large floorcloth, do it a section at a time, then mix new dye and continue.

4 Place wax paper under the floorcloth. Use a 1-inch (2.5 cm) brush to wax over the octagonal shapes, covering the turquoise and bright green areas. Outline the motifs first and then fill in the middle (photo B).

5 Now, carefully turn the canvas over, replace the wax paper, and brush wax on the back if the first application didn't thoroughly penetrate the canvas (photo C).

6 Place the canvas on heavy plastic sheeting, then mix the final dyebath.

7 Use this last color to brush across the entire front of the floorcloth (photo D). Turn the cloth over and brush across the back until it's completely saturated. Cover it with plastic (to keep it from drying out) and leave it to sit for 2 hours. Then, rinse and boil as needed, and hang to air dry.

TIP

TURN THE WAX UP HOTTER THAN USUAL SO IT PENETRATES THIS THICK FABRIC; TRY AN ADDITIONAL 25°F (4°C).

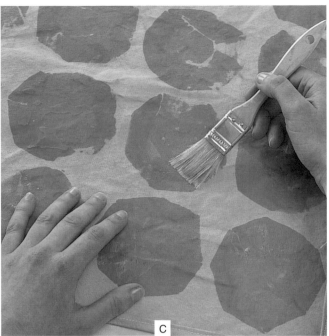

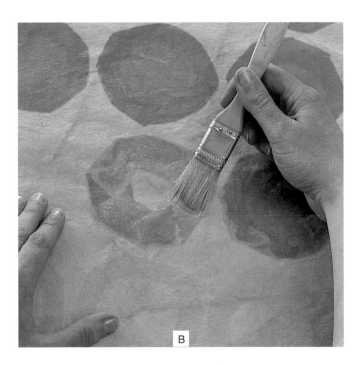

Wren T-Shirt

Paint and overdye to imitate block printing when you embellish a T-shirt with this colorful group of birds.

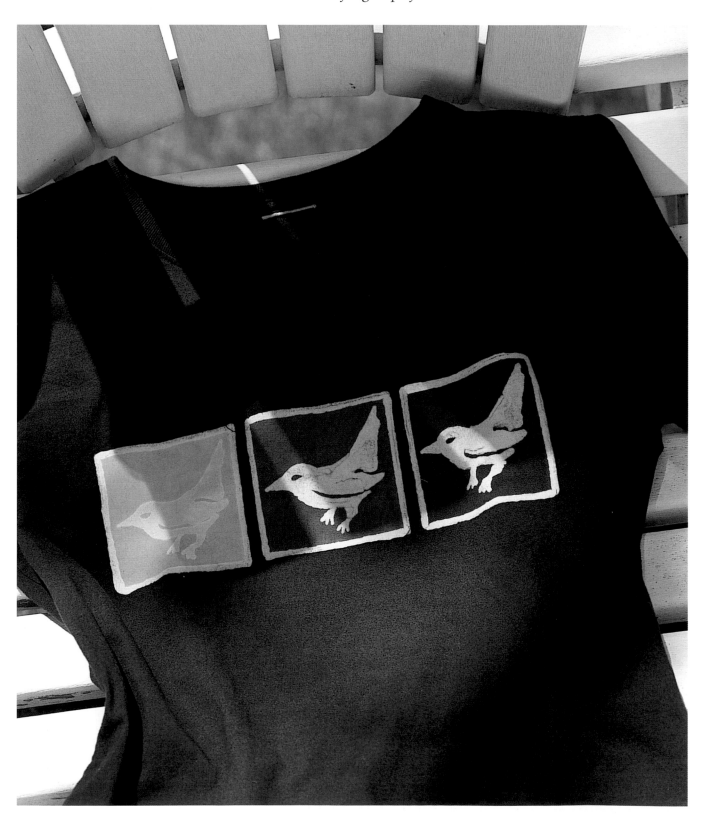

MATERIALS

Essential supplies (page 20)

Paper

Ruler

Pencil

Template (page 74)

Blank fitted T-shirt (cotton knit)

Black permanent marker

Scissors

Rinse cup and water

Paper towels

DYEBATH 1

$^1/_2$ tsp (1.5 g) golden yellow dye

1 tsp (7 g) salt

$^1/_2$ tsp (2 g) washing soda

$^1/_4$ c (60 mL) water

$^1/_4$ tsp (750 mg) rust orange dye

1 tsp (7 g) salt

$^1/_2$ tsp (2 g) washing soda

$^1/_4$ cup (60 mL) water

$^1/_2$ tsp (1.5 g) wine dye

1 tsp (7 g) salt

$^1/_2$ tsp (2 g) washing soda

$^1/_4$ cup (60 mL) water

DYEBATH 2

12 Tbsp (108 g) black dye

6 c (2064 g) salt

$2^1/_4$ c (378 g) washing soda

3 gal (11.4 L) water

Rinse, boil, wash, and dry.

1 Make a paper guide to mark the location of each square; this shirt has a 10 x 3-inch (25.4 x 7.6 cm) paper guide, with $^1/_2$ inch (1.3 cm) of space between the 3-inch (7.6 cm) squares. Center the paper guide on the shirt, then use a water-soluble marker to designate the corners of each square (photo A). Remove the paper and use the marker and ruler to connect the dots into three squares.

2 Trace the bird template onto another piece of paper and trace over the lines with the black marker. Cut it out, place it inside the shirt, and trace a bird into each square, using a water-soluble marker (photo B).

3 After you've traced the last bird, cover a piece of cardboard with wax paper, secure it with tape, and insert it into the shirt. Add a protective border of wax around the squares, about 2 inches (5 cm) wide. Begin by outlining the squares with the tjanting, then filling in with a brush. Cover the $^1/_2$-inch (1.3 cm) space between the squares, too.

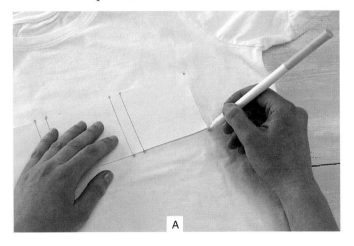

A

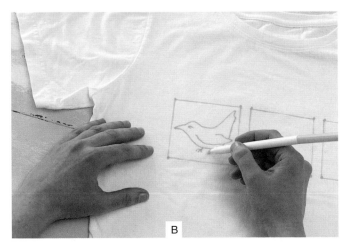

B

4 Use the tjanting to fill in each bird shape, but leave unwaxed the line of each bird's wing and eye (photo C).

5 In preparation for painting, make three separate dye mixes as directed. Wait to add the soda until just before painting, and be sure to stir it into the mixture—if you shake it, it'll become too foamy to use.

6 Brush each square with a separate dye color (photo D). Leave to dry completely, overnight if necessary. Be sure to rinse the brush between colors, and use a paper towel to catch drips.

7 Remove the cardboard and boil as necessary, then dry. Replace the wax paper and insert cardboard again. Wax over the squares completely, adding a narrow border around each square. Carefully turn the shirt inside out (so you don't crack the wax) and wax the back of the squares, too. (This prevents any excess dye from bleeding through to the front of the design.) Remove the cardboard. Finally, overdye and finish as indicated. Be sure to rinse well.

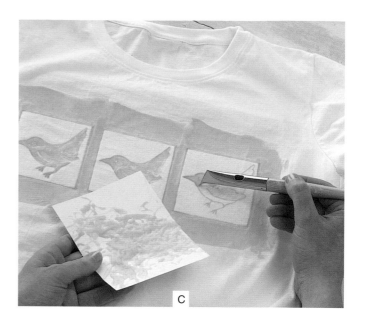

C

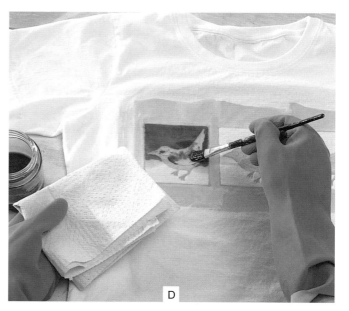

D

NOTE

DIFFERENT DYES MAY REACT TO THIS TECHNIQUE DIFFERENTLY. HERE, THE ORANGE DYE WAS STABLE AFTER THE FIRST DYEBATH, WHILE THE YELLOW AND RED DYES BOTH BLED A LITTLE ONTO THE SHIRT. BE SURE TO CHOOSE A DARKER COLOR FOR THE OVERDYE STEP IN CASE YOU NEED TO CAMOUFLAGE ANY STAINS.

Abstract Card

Let your imagination guide the tjanting when you design these cards that feature gleaming silk inserts.

MATERIALS

Essential supplies (page 20)

Wooden frame

Silk pins

Silk charmeuse fabric

Rinse cup

Cotton swabs

Card with a blank window (or card stock, craft knife, ruler, pencil, and cutting mat)

Fabric scissors

Toothpick

Craft glue

1 Cover the wooden frame with masking tape so the dye won't absorb into the wood. Use the silk pins to stretch the fabric onto the frame.

2 Use a tjanting to draw abstract shapes and dots, (photo A). Have fun and don't be afraid to be creative in this step!

3 Mix very small amounts of your chosen dye colors; add some dye, some salt, and some soda in the water and mix well. (Stir in the soda, so the dye doesn't foam.) Use more dye for darker colors, and add water to lighten colors. Exact amounts aren't too important in this project; less than $^1/_4$ teaspoon each of dye (750 mg), salt (5 g), and washing soda (3 g) were used per each $^1/_4$ cup (60 mL) water. Remember that the colors will look darker when they're wet.

4 Apply the dye as you choose, but be sure to rinse the brush between each application of a new color. You'll be able to see when the painted dye has saturated the fabric (photo B).

5 You can mix colors right on the silk. For instance, paint with blue, rinse the brush, and add a little yellow for a blue-green. Add even more yellow for chartreuse. Play with the colors and tilt the frame to get the colors to run together, if desired. If little pools of dye form that you want to remove, use cotton swabs to pull the dye off the cloth (photo C).

6 Let the silk dry, then remove it from the frame and boil it as needed. Wash and dry.

7 Now place the silk on the card. If you choose to make your own card, cut and fold the card stock as desired, then cut a window with the craft knife. Place the silk behind the window and move it around a bit until you're pleased with the surface design you see. Cut out this piece of silk, making sure its dimensions are a little bigger than the window.

8 Use a toothpick or similar tool to apply a small amount of glue around the opening on the wrong side of the window and attach the silk (photo D). Let the card dry completely.

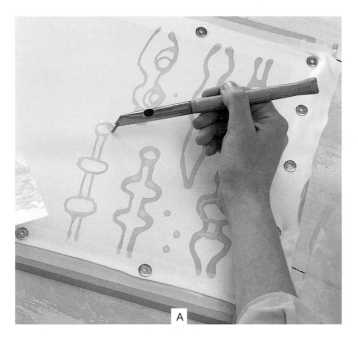

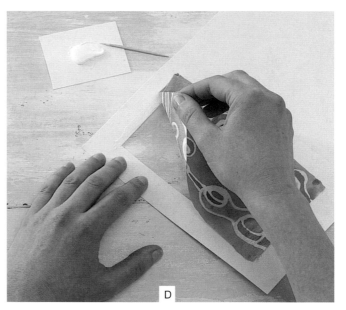

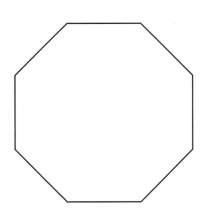

Enlarge as needed.

Wren T-shirt, page 68

Fantastic Floorcloth, page 65

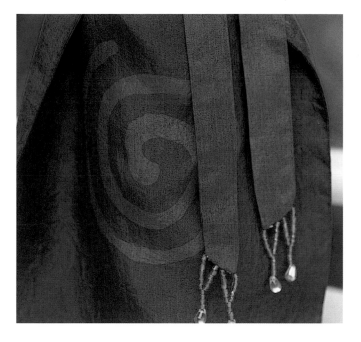

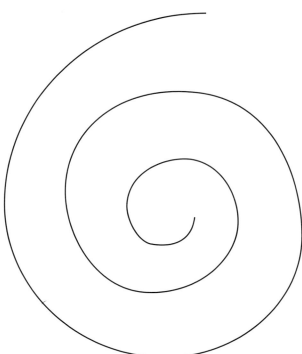

Enlarge as needed.

Wine Gift Bag, page 52

Enlarge as needed.

Triptych Wall Hanging, page 56

Bathing Suit, page 28

GALLERY OF PATTERNS

Here's a collection of the stamped patterns used in the book. Remember that you can use just about any pattern on just about any project.

Scarves, page 32—wooden block

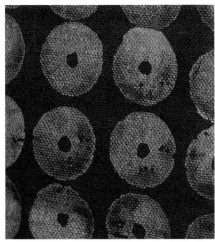

Lunch bag, page 22—wooden spool

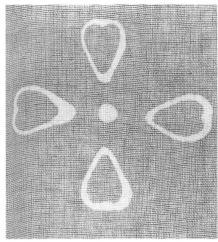

Curtains, page 24—wooden dowel and cookie cutter

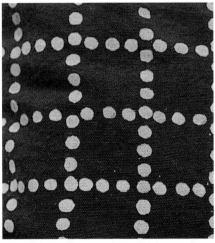

Envelope pillows, page 26—wooden dowel

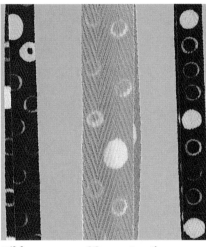

Ribbons, page 30—pastry tip

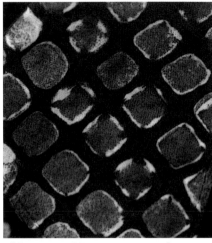

Shirt, page 35—square wooden dowel

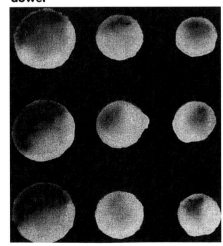

Dog bed, page 38—wooden dowels and spools

Top, page 40—cookie cutters

Slipcovers, page 42—wooden dowels

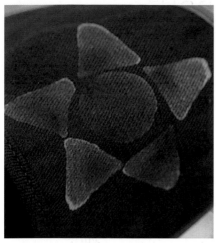

Shoes, page 46—wooden dowels

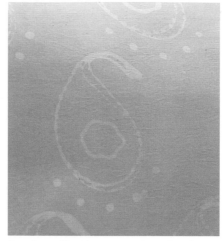

Paisley pillows, page 48—wire tjap, cookie cutter, and wooden dowel

Sconce, page 62—tjanting, cookie cutter, and wooden dowel

Linens, page 59—square wooden dowel

ACKNOWLEDGMENTS

THANK YOU, thank you to these fine folks, my friends and family: Katie Moor; Robin Original, Batik Queen; Jamie House; Alan, Richard, Dorothy, and Karen Light; Mr. Billy; Catherine Cornell and Bill Drinkard; and the Waterbearers (you know who you are!).

Thanks to these people at Lark Books: Valerie Shrader, Paige Gilchrist, Carol Taylor, Rosemary Kast, Jeff Hamilton, and Dana Irwin. And thanks to Sandra Stambaugh, for the pretty pictures.

Batik by Robin Original

A special thank you to Cathy and Larry Sklar at The Albemarle Inn in Asheville, N.C., our beautiful location for the project photographs throughout this book. They can be reached at: 800-621-7435 or www.albemar-leinn.com.

A NOTE ABOUT SUPPLIERS

Usually, the supplies you need for making the projects in Lark books can be found at your local craft supply store, discount mart, home improvement center, or retail shop relevant to the topic of the book. Occasionally, however, you may need to buy materials or tools from specialty suppliers. In order to provide you with the most up-to-date information, we have created a list of suppliers on our Web site, which we update on a regular basis. Visit us at www.larkbooks.com, click on "Craft Supply Sources," and then click on the relevant topic. You will find numerous companies listed with their web address and/or mailing address and phone number.

INDEX